T0094700

Dear Reader,

We're excited to introduce you to this wonderful book about mammals, part of our Beginnings collection. These beautifully illustrated, information-packed titles introduce youngsters to the fascinating world of animals, and, by extension, to themselves.

Scientific curiosity begins in childhood, with young minds thirstily absorbing information about the world around them. Exposure to animals—whether in nature or in a book—is often at the root of a child's interest in science. Young Jane Goodall loved to observe the wildlife near her home, a passion that inspired her groundbreaking chimpanzee research. Charles Turner spent hours reading about ants in the pages of his father's books before growing into a trailblazing entomologist. Spark curiosity in a child and watch them develop a lifelong enthusiasm for learning.

Beginnings books encourage children to make real-world connections that sharpen their analytical skills and give them a head start in STEM (science, technology, engineering, and math). Research shows that young children who are exposed to nonfiction develop strong vocabulary and reading comprehension skills, later translating to higher rates of student achievement.

More than an educational primer, these stories also illustrate and explore caring love in animal families. Showing children this type of attachment in the natural world fosters empathy, kindness, and compassion in both their interpersonal and interspecies interactions.

An easy choice for the home, library, or classroom, our Beginnings collection has something to spark or sustain budding curiosity in any child.

Enjoy!

Dia

Dia L. Michels
Publisher, Science Naturally

Beginnings

P.S. Our supplemental learning materials enable adults to support young readers in their quest for knowledge. Check them out, free of charge, at ScienceNaturally.com.

For the grown-ups everywhere who help babies grow
-Dia L. Michels

For Adelaide Stephenson Davies
-Wesley Davies

This Is How I GROW

By Dia L. Michels

Illustrated by Wesley Davies

Science, Naturally!
An imprint of Platypus Media, LLC
Washington, D.C.

This Is How I Grow
Hardback ISBN 13: 978-1-938492-10-5 | First Edition • March 2020
Paperback ISBN 13: 978-1-938492-08-2 | First Edition • March 2020
eBook ISBN 13: 978-1-938492-09-9 | First Edition • March 2020
Part of the Platypus Media collection, Beginnings
Beginnings logo by Hannah Thelen, © 2018 Platypus Media

Written by Dia L. Michels, Text © 2020
Illustrated by Wesley Davies, Illustrations © 2020
Globe Illustration by Hannah Thelen © Science, Naturally! 2020

Project Manager: Anna Cohen, Washington, DC
Cover and Book Design: Hannah Thelen, Washington, DC
        Victoria Stingo, Washington, DC
        and Wesley Davies, Providence, RI

Teacher's Guide available at the Educational Resources page of ScienceNaturally.com.

Published by:
        Science, Naturally! - An imprint of Platypus Media, LLC
        725 8th Street, SE
        Washington, DC 20003
        202-465-4798 • Toll-free 1-866-SCI-9876 (1-866-724-9876)
        Info@ScienceNaturally.com • www.ScienceNaturally.com

Distributed to the book trade by:
        National Book Network
        301-459-3366 • Toll-free: 1-800-787-6859
        CustServ@NBNbooks.com • www.NBNbooks.com

Library of Congress Control Number: 2019041111 (print) | 2019041112 (ebook)

10 9 8 7 6 5 4 3 2 1

The front cover may be reproduced freely, without modification, for review or non-commercial educational purposes.

All rights reserved. No part of this book may be reproduced in any form without the express written permission of the publisher. Front cover exempted (see above).

Printed in Canada.

Contents

E Endangered Species   **V** Vulnerable Species

Where Do You Grow?

AFRICA

ANTARCTICA

ASIA

AUSTRALIA

EUROPE

NORTH AMERICA

SOUTH AMERICA

I am a pup,
a Brazilian free-tailed bat baby.

I grow up in a dark, dark cave.

I could not see much, but I could smell my mother. While I nursed, she cleaned me and learned my scent.

When I was full, she took me to the
cave ceiling to hang with the other pups.
She came back twice each day to feed me.

Now that I am four weeks old, I drop from the top of the cave, spread my wings, and fly. I practice with the other pups.

When I am six weeks old, I will not need my
mother's milk anymore. I will fly through
the forest, catching crunchy bugs,
and I will be all grown up.

I am a kit, a red squirrel baby.

I grow up with my siblings, high in a tree.

We were born bald and blind. Every two hours, we curled up with our mother to nurse.

Sometimes she left us sleeping while she went out to find food.

When we were a month old, we finally opened our eyes and stood up.

Now that we are six weeks old,
we don't nurse as often.

Our mother shows us which nuts
and berries are best to eat.

When I am ten weeks old,
I will know how to find my own food
and hide some for later, and I will
be all grown up.

I am a joey, a red kangaroo baby.

I grow up safe in my mother's pouch.
I was born as small as a jellybean.

I climbed into my mother's pouch
where I lived for six months.
I nursed the whole time.

When I was strong
enough, I lifted my head
out of my mother's pouch
for my first look at the world.

I jump out of the pouch and explore.

I nibble on the same grasses that my mother eats. Now I only nurse two times a day.

When I am a year old,
I will stay outside
of my mother's pouch.

I will sleep in the shade
and search for food in the bushes,
and I will be all grown up.

I am a cub, a cougar baby.

I grow up hidden in a den.

When I was born I could not see or hear, but I could feel my brothers and sisters around me.

Sometimes our mother left the cave to hunt,
but she always came back to feed us.

After ten days, we opened our eyes and
began to explore.

After three months, we practice hunting on our mother's kills.

As we get stronger, we will nurse less and spend some nights alone.

When I am a year and a half old, I will wander far away from my family to find my own home. I will be able to hunt for my own food, and I will be all grown up.

I am a calf, a blue whale baby.

I grow up on the move.

As soon as I was born, I followed my mother as she swam through the warm tropical waters.

When I got hungry,
I poked her with my nose
and she squirted her milk into
the water for me. I drink 375 liters
of milk every day to fatten up fast.

When I am three months old, it is time for us to travel south. I will make this long journey every year.

When we finally arrive in the cold Antarctic waters, my mother shows me how to feast on krill.

When I am two years old, I will be able to travel by myself, and I will be all grown up.

I am a cub, a polar bear baby.

I grow up in a cave under the snow.

After my twin and I were born, we snuggled close to our mother and nursed.

When we were a month old,
we first opened our eyes.
We were starting to grow
big and strong.

Over a few months, we
grew thick, warm coats.
Finally, our mother led
us out into the cold.

For two years, we watch our mother hunt on the sea ice and try to copy her.

Soon, she will leave us alone and we will have to find our own food.

When I am three years old, I will be
a fierce hunter. I will weigh 270 kilograms
and I will be all grown up.

I am a calf, a Masai giraffe baby.

I grow up tall.

Right after I was born, I wobbled to my feet so I could reach high enough to nurse.

For a few months,
my mother's milk was my only food.

I followed her everywhere the herd went,
and I nursed whenever I was hungry.

After a few months, my mother teaches me to pull leaves off of trees with my long tongue.

Soon, I will chew 34 kilograms of plants every day.

When I turn four years old, I will be
taller than any other land animal!

My eyes will be strong enough to
see predators from miles away,
and I will be all grown up.

**I am a calf,
an Asian elephant baby.**

I grow up very, very slowly.

After I was born, I followed my mother wherever
she went, and drank her milk whenever I could.

After a few months, I started following other moms in our herd, nursing from anyone who would let me.

Now I'm six months old.

I can use my trunk to tickle my mother, cover myself in cool mud, and pull food into my mouth. The adults in my herd show me which grasses to eat.

When I am five years old, I will play an important role in my community. I will look out for the smaller members of my herd, and I will be all grown up.

This Is **Where I Grow**

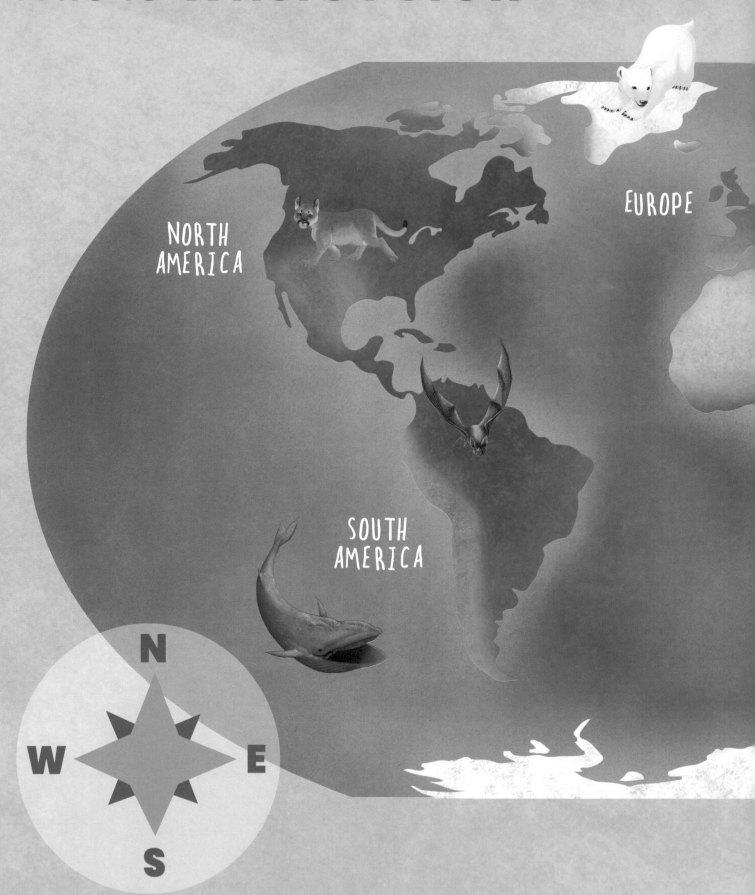

EUROPE

NORTH
AMERICA

SOUTH
AMERICA

N

W · E

S

ASIA

AFRICA

AUSTRALIA

ANTARCTICA

Where do *you* grow?

Resources

We relied on a number of resources when researching the animals and habitats in this book. Here are the main sources we used to gather our information. Check them out to learn more!

• **American Society of Mammalogists**, a society of scientists devoted to studying mammals and publishers of the Journal of Mammalogy (Mammalogy.org)

• **Animal Diversity Web**, a database of animal natural history, distribution, classification, and conservation biology from the University of Michigan (AnimalDiversity.org)

• **The Encyclopedia Britannica**, the world's oldest general knowledge English-language encyclopedia (Britannica.com)

• **The International Union for Conservation of Nature's Red List of Threatened Species**, a comprehensive compilation of information on the global conservation status of animal, fungi, and plant species (IUCNRedList.org)

• **National Geographic**, a global nonprofit dedicated to helping understand the world and generating solutions for a more sustainable future (NationalGeographic.org)

• **Nature Works**, an online resource developed by New Hampshire PBS in collaboration with the Squam Lakes Natural Science Center (NHPTV.org)

• **San Diego Zoo**, a conservation organization committed to saving species around the world (Zoo.SanDiegoZoo.org)

• **The Smithsonian National Museum of Natural History**, an organization devoted to understanding the natural world and our place in it (NaturalHistory.si.edu)

• **Western Wildlife Outreach**, a science-based community education project specializing in large carnivores of the Western United States (WesternWildlife.org)

• **The World Wildlife Foundation**, the leading agency working to protect nature and the future of our planet (WorldWildlife.org)

Special thanks to Don Wilson and Michael L. Power for their expert input.

Download the free Teacher's Guide for a full resource list, more information, and hands-on activities about the animals in this book.

Access it at ScienceNaturally.com/Educational-Recources.

TG Look for this symbol throughout the rest of the book, which indicates that a related activity can be found in the Teacher's Guide.

About the Author

Dia L. Michels is an award-winning science and parenting writer who has authored or edited over a dozen books for both children and adults. This is her fourth book exploring science topics through animal stories. Studying mammals has helped her appreciate the simplicity and importance of attachment parenting and breastfeeding. The mother of three grown children, she lives in Washington D.C., where she shares her home with three cats and a dog. She can be reached at Dia@ScienceNaturally.com.

About the Illustrator

Wesley Davies is an artist from New England who specializes in illustration and comic art. He received a Bachelor of Arts in anthropology from Kenyon College, earning Phi Beta Kappa honors, and has been making art all his life. He provided spot drawings for Platypus Media's 2018 publication *Babies Nurse*, but this book marks his debut as a children's book illustrator. He lives in Rhode Island on occupied Naragansett land with his growing collection of houseplants. He can be reached at WesDavies.com or by email at Wesley@ScienceNaturally.com.

About Wesley's Process

Visual authenticity is essential when creating a science book because there's so much you can learn from looking at the pictures—what an animal looks like, how the family group is structured, what plants and other animals are in their environment, how big the animals are, and much more. We asked Wesley how he researched and made his art for *This Is How I Grow*.

For me, drawing is about two things: observation and consideration. First, I have to look at the subject I am going to draw or paint so that I understand what it looks like and how it moves, and then I have to figure out how to put that movement on the page.

The first thing I do when I'm going to start an illustration is gather references such as pictures, videos, or books that I find online or at the local public library. Sometimes I already know about an animal or environment because I have seen that animal before in the wild, at zoos, or wildlife sanctuaries. I will also gather references on where a subject lives and what the environment is like there. Once I have enough information, I will do some practice sketches or studies of the subject in a sketchbook or digitally on my computer tablet, which is where I do most of my drawing and painting. I try to keep these sketches simple and quick so I can get a feel for the basic shapes that make up each animal's form, and will make note of small details to remember for later.

Next, I will plan out a rough version of the illustration. This rough version is monochromatic (all done in many shades of the same color) to help me understand how I want the composition to look with light and shadow. This rough version will go through many revisions, and once it looks and feels right, I start to add details. When this is done, I add in blocks of color to the animals, which I will later paint over and refine. Having multiple layers of paint also adds to the richness and luminosity of the color, although I have to be careful not to add too much and accidentally make the colors muddy. As I finish the background, I adjust the colors and shading on the subjects so they are more cohesive, and after I have done more revisions and checked over the illustrations for mistakes, the pieces will be finished.

What did you learn from looking at the pictures in the book? What questions do you have about what you saw? Some of your questions may be answered on the following pages...

Brazilian Free-Tailed Bats
Tadarida brasiliensis

"How does the baby stay upside down with its mom?"

Most bats hang upside down when they're not flying. Their feet are specially evolved to make holding on while they hang as easy as sitting is for us. When the baby settles into the bat nursery with all of the other pups, it will hang upside down too, but while it's with its mom, the bat pup grasps snugly on to her fur with its tiny talons.

 See the Teacher's Guide for an activity demonstrating how bats hang upside down so easily.

"Are those bats too?"

No, they're red-tailed hawks! Hawks are actually predators of bats and are active at dusk, when Brazilian free-tailed bats start leaving their cave to hunt. Even though the bats are going out to find their own food, they have to make sure that they don't end up as dinner themselves!

There are two other Brazilian free-tailed bat predators on the same page as the hawks. Can you find them?

"Where are the bat babies?"

Baby bats stay inside the cave where their predators can't get to them. They only leave once they learn how to fly. The cave is naturally cold, but the pups are clumped together for warmth. They stay safely inside the cave until they're strong enough fliers to give them a fighting chance at escaping predators.

Red Squirrels
Sciurus vulgaris

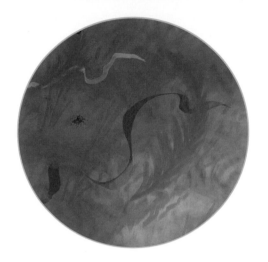

"Why are there ribbons in the nest?"

Red squirrels eat, sleep, and raise their young inside their nests. They use moss, leaves, grass, bark, and any other materials they can find to make their nest. Because they live so close to humans, they often take discarded human-made materials for their nests, including paper, shoelaces, and ribbons.

"Do babies fall out of the hole in the tree?"

Red squirrel babies start moving around before they even open their eyes. Even though they can't see where they're going, they usually don't fall. Once they start moving around, they use their tiny claws to hang on to the edge of the nest or the outside of the tree to keep them securely in place.

Sometimes an unlucky red squirrel does fall out of its nest. If you find a squirrel baby who doesn't seem injured, you can be pretty confident that the mom will come find it. Give it something to help keep warm and wait for its mother to return.

"Do the squirrels get along with the birds?"

Birds and red squirrels don't get along. In fact, birds are predators. Big birds like hawks and eagles capture and eat young squirrels. Adult squirrels raid birds' nests for eggs to eat, and even eat newborn birds. This isn't a squirrel's favorite meal, but they will eat birds when they're desperate for food.

Red Kangaroos
Macropus rufus

"Why is the mom licking her stomach?"

After giving birth, a mother kangaroo licks a path along her stomach for her newborn to follow into her pouch. A newborn kangaroo is blind, but it can smell where its mother's tongue has been. It doesn't have back legs yet, so it pulls itself along that path with its tiny arms and into its mother's pouch.

"Why are their feet so big?"

Red kangaroos use their big feet in lots of ways besides just getting around. They can't move their back legs one at a time, so they always hop instead of walk. When they sense danger approaching, they will loudly thump their feet on the ground to warn their family.

Did you know that red kangaroos are part of the Macropus family? This word literally means "big feet."

"What's that baby doing?"

That joey is nursing. A female kangaroo's nipples are inside of her pouch. When the babies are really little, they live and eat there, but once they are older, they live outside; however, they still need to nurse. So, older red kangaroo babies stick their heads back inside the pouch to eat.

Cougars
Puma concolor

"Why are the babies spotted when the mom isn't?"

Baby cougars are born with spots that they use to blend into their surroundings. The spotting looks like the shadows inside of the cave or through the leaves of trees in the forest. Fully grown cougars don't have many predators, but the babies are more vulnerable to attack by bears, wolves, and even birds of prey. This is why their moms keep them hidden in caves or other kinds of shelters until they're big enough to protect themselves.

"Why aren't the other deer running away?"

It's true that cougars prey on deer; the animal that they are eating in the foreground of this picture is also a deer. However, it's because of the presence of that meal that these deer don't have too much to worry about. It takes a lot of energy to attack and kill any large, fast animal, and energy comes from eating. Because this cougar mom and her cubs already have plenty to eat, it would be a waste of energy to attempt another kill.

"Are they going to eat the whole deer at once?"

Cougars don't eat that much food all in one sitting. Adults eat about 4.5 kilograms of meat every day, and cubs eat even less. When a cougar makes a kill, they hide the body somewhere where other animals won't find it. They cover it with leaves, branches, dirt, and/or snow to keep it hidden, and come back each day to eat a little more. A single adult cougar can make one deer last more than a week!

Blue Whales
Balaenoptera musculus

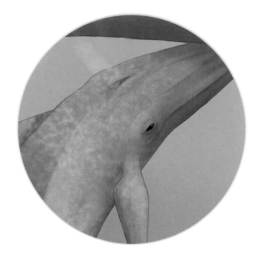

"Why is there a hole on the top of their head?"

Just like humans, whales breathe air. Instead of using their mouth or nose, whales breathe through a hole on the top of their head called a blowhole, which is similar to a human nostril. It's easier to stick the blowhole out of the water than it would be to lift their whole head.

Because they live underwater, whales can hold their breath for a long, long time. Blue whales can stay underwater for 20 minutes at a time.

"What are those white dots on the whales?"

Those are barnacles! Barnacles are small creatures that live inside of shells. They attach themselves to whales, boats, and other underwater surfaces with a strong glue that they produce. They like living on whales, because they need to move quickly through the water to eat. As the whale swims, the barnacles filter the water that passes over them for food.

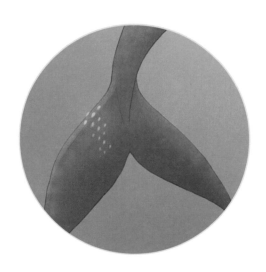

"What's in the baby whale's mouth?"

Instead of having teeth, blue whales have baleen, which is like thick hair that hangs down from the whale's jaw. They use it to strain and collect food. Whales take in a big mouthful of ocean water that contains krill and small fish. They push out the water while their baleen traps the food inside.

TG To learn more about baleen and how they work, check the Teacher's Guide.

Polar Bears
Ursus maritimus

"What does the mom eat inside the cave?"

Polar bear moms eat a lot of food while pregnant. However, after giving birth they don't eat anything at all for about three months. They have to wait for their babies to grow strong enough to venture outside. Then, mom finally catches a seal to eat. This is one of the longest periods of time that any animal goes without food!

"How do polar bears catch seals?"

Polar bears use their strong sense of smell and their powerful claws to catch seals. They find holes in the sea ice and wait. Polar bears can smell seals under the ice. When a seal comes close, they swipe a paw down and pull it out of the water.

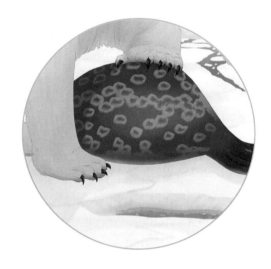

"What's that?"

That is an arctic fox. These small animals live in very cold environments. Their white fur helps them blend into the snow. It's hard for such small animals to find food in the arctic. They often wait for polar bears to finish their meal so they can eat the leftovers.

Polar bears mostly only eat the fatty parts of the seals they catch, leaving the meat available for scavengers like arctic foxes.

Masai Giraffes
Giraffa camelopardalis tippelskirchii

"What is that baby doing?"

Giraffes drink out of big pools of water in the ground called watering holes. Because they are so tall, and have such long necks, they have to spread their front legs apart and lean their heads down to take a drink. But they have to be careful; crocodiles live in the watering hole.

Did you know that adult giraffes don't have many predators? Only calves have to worry about getting attacked by a crocodile. Even lions will only attack an adult giraffe if they are starving.

"Why is her tongue purple?"

When giraffes eat, they wrap their long tongue around a branch and strip off the leaves. The dark blue color of their tongue helps prevent sunburn. Many of the plants they eat have spikey thorns, but the giraffes' thick tongues and sticky spit keep them from getting hurt.

"Why are they fighting?"

Male giraffes fight each each other using their long, strong necks. This behavior is called "necking." Calves will do this for fun or play, but adult giraffes take it more seriously. Necking establishes dominance and determines who gets to mate. After fighting, Masai giraffes will often make up by cuddling with one another.

Asian Elephants
Elephas maximus

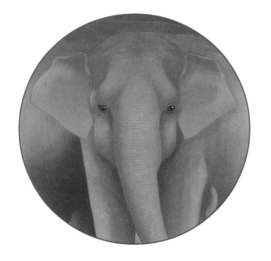

"Why don't the Asian elephants have tusks?"

Only male Asian elephants have tusks, and herds are made up entirely of related female elephants and their calves. However, some of the females do have small teeth called *tushes* that look like tusks. These teeth are softer, smaller, and do not stick far out of their mouth. They may be used to strip bark off of trees to eat, but are not long enough to be used for digging, lifting, or fighting, like a male's tusks.

 See the Teacher's Guide for an activity that demonstrates one very important way Asian elephants use their tusks.

"Is that animal going to attack the elephants? "

We usually think of bears as scary predators, but that little guy is a sloth bear, one of the smallest members of the bear family. These bears weigh less than 115 kilograms, so they wouldn't be much of a match for an Asian elephant. Sloth bears eat both meat and vegetation, but they mostly just eat termites. In fact, sloth bears are more likely to be attacked by an elephant than to attack one.

"Do elephants eat and drink through their trunk?"

Elephants use their trunks to pick up food and water, but they don't eat or drink through their trunk. Their trunk is like a combination nose and upper lip, and it's very strong and flexible. Just like people, elephants eat and drink through their mouths—but their trunks help like a hand or arm.

Baby Asian elephants suck on the tip of their trunk the same way that human babies suck on their thumb or a pacifier. It helps keep them calm and content.

More Books from the Beginnings Collection

Cuddled and Carried

Cuddled and Carried
Consentido y cargado

Celebrate the special bond between parent and child in the animal kingdom.

32 pages each • Recommended for ages 0–4

ENGLISH
8.5 x 11"
Hardback ($14.95) ISBN 13: 978-1-930775-99-2
Paperback ($9.95) ISBN 13: 978-1-930775-98-5
eBook ($8.99) ISBN 13: 978-1-930775-43-5

BILINGUAL (English/Spanish)
8.5 x 11"
Hardback ($14.95) ISBN 13: 978-1-930775-96-1
Paperback ($9.95) ISBN 13: 978-1-930775-95-4
eBook ($8.99) ISBN 13: 978-1-930775-97-8

BILINGUAL (English/Spanish)
Stroller-bag edition - 6 x 8"
Paperback ($8.95) ISBN 13: 978-1-930775-65-7
eBook ($7.99) ISBN 13: 978-1-930775-66-4

Babies Nurse

Babies Nurse
Así se alimentan los bebés

Sweet poetry and stunning watercolors introduce readers to mammal mothers nursing their young.

32 pages each • Recommended for ages 4–7

ENGLISH
8.5 x 11"
Hardback ($14.95) ISBN 13: 978-1-930775-61-9
Paperback ($9.95) ISBN 13: 978-1-930775-71-8
eBook ($8.99) ISBN 13: 978-1-930775-36-7

BILINGUAL (English/Spanish)
8.5 x 11"
Hardback ($14.95) ISBN 13: 978-1-930775-73-2
Paperback ($9.95) ISBN 13: 978-1-930775-72-5
eBook ($8.99) ISBN 13: 978-1-930775-74-9

If My Mom Were a Platypus:
Mammal Babies and Their Mothers

Si mi mamá fuera un ornitorrinco:
Los bebés mamíferos y sus madres

Discover how 14 mammal babies navigate the path from helplessness to maturity.

64 pages each • Recommended for ages 8–12

ENGLISH
7 x 10"
Paperback ($12.95) ISBN 13: 978-1-938492-11-2
eBook ($8.99) ISBN 13: 978-1-938492-12-9
Also available in Hebrew and Dutch

SPANISH
8.5 x 11"
Hardback ($16.95) ISBN 13: 978-1-938492-03-7
Paperback ($12.95) ISBN 13: 978-1-938492-06-8
eBook ($11.99) ISBN 13: 978-1-938492-05-1

Science, Naturally!
Sparking curiosity through reading

Free downloadable Teacher's Guides available at ScienceNaturally.com